# JOURNEY

## BEE COLTSON

ARPress

**ARPress**
45 Dan Road Suite 36
Canton MA 02021

Hotline:   1(800) 220-7660
Fax:        1(855) 752-6001

Ordering Information:
Quantity Sales. Special discounts are available on quantity purchases by corporations, associations, and others. For details, contact the publisher at the address above.

Printed in the United States of America.

| ISBN-13 | Paperback | 979-8-89389-754-8 |
|---------|-----------|-------------------|
|         | eBook     | 979-8-89389-755-5 |

Library of Congress Control Number: 2024922621

# Contents

*For my parents, Hoyt and Bea Ayers, who set me on the path.*

*For my sons, Scott and Eric, who showed me the way.*

*And for John who waited for me.*

*All I am is written here –*
*A gift for you.*
*To be read with eyes that are wiser*
*for having seen*
*the disappointment of dreams*
*that don't come true.*
*And the simple joy of just a few*
*that do.*

# Travel

I shut my suit case and my heart
By standing on them.
And find I travel faster when I leave
My winter coats and heavy hopes
At home.

# Souvenirs

*Holding onto shiny things*
*Smooth stones, marigolds,*
*Finding shells and wondering where*
*To hide them.*

*Words of longing scattered*
*On a green and yellow field,*
*Letting go to have the wind*
*Decide them.*

# Tranquility

You are tranquil waters in the bay.
I should not disturb you but I do –
Casting a small stone to see the ripples grow
And watch the smooth confusion.
They are not waves.
I am not the tide.
I'm but a weary watcher of the bay,
Victim of the ocean's roll and sway,
Longing for tranquility.

You do not rise nor bid me stay.
But I can see that you are moved.

# Tourist

Your arms were not my destination.
Your smile was never mentioned on my chart.
Losing some part
Of my life here
Was not my plan.

The lines around your eyes were etched there
By laughing at travelers who lose their way
And come inside
To ask direction
And believe your lies.

I've been to Paradise –
Me, the tourist,
You, the guide.

# Journey

The longest journey is not far
Distance-wise.
It can be just beyond your smiles
Or through the endless miles
Of your eyes.

# *Who*

Who will love us when we part
Going your way, going mine.
Who will turn the latch and start
Evening fires of oak and pine.

Who will tend the hearth and heart,
Light the candle, serve the wine.
Who will love us when we part
Going your way, going mine.

# Time

Hold this day while the sun is setting
Gently In your hand.
For time slips through like sand
More slowly when you do not hold too tight.

We cannot live forever by the sea.
Even the sun will be exhausted and the night
Will know us last.

Hold this day gently and think of me.
There will be time for forgetting
When Iam gone.
And darkness falls
Finally
And fast.

# Bits of String

I save our torn pieces of time together
Like bits of string
Bound neatly
Put away
For no reason whatsoever.

Tomorrow may bring
Some greater need than today.
And I shall weave then
A lovely thing
From these frayed and tattered
Bits of string.

# Infinity

The space that separates the stars
Is where the sorrow goes
And that is why
I suppose
The creator made the sky.

We need infinity
For love's debris.

# Rejection

Pushedaway,
A gentle but certain shove.
I understand,
Let go the hand
That once reached out for love.

# Ending

You are telling me to go
to go
I hear the words
the words
echo.

You are saying goodbye

And I'll never know
never know
never know
why.

# *Portrait*

Taken for granted the portrait–
You admire the frame.

I am more than the edges and corners of your world.

And I belong, not necessarily to the buyer,
But to the one who can see
The silkscreen canvas where I sign my name
And the sea-spray color that is me.

# This Day

Together on a sunny bank–
White October clouds
Glad to bring their blessing,
Warm October wind caressing
This place we share.

You read my book of verses
While I read your face.
I look away
And send a silent prayer
To thank
Some sympathetic god
For this day.

# The Cherry Tree

The cherry tree was beautiful yesterday
Before the storm stripped the blossoms from her fragile
branches And tossed them to the ground.
The tree still stands and a few pale petals hang on.
Compared to the extravagant dress she proudly wore
She appears ashamed in these faded ruined rags.
Next spring might bring another chance for her to bloom—
But knowing there are just somany springs
And how much effort is required
To risk opening her heart to April winds,
I dare not hope.

*What the storm has done to the cherry tree.*
*This is what you have done to me.*

# Rehearsal

Trying to prepare
For the day when you go
Is like deciding
What to say
To God
When I die.

If the door to Heaven is open
I 'll have to say
That I
Have been there.

And when He offers Hell
I'll have to tell
That I have been there too.

There will be no
Place for me
Even then
When
You
Go.

# Rain

In the end I notice rainbows
And wonder if the dark enduring pain
Is worth this small comfort.

Time passes, clouds gather,
And in the distance,
Rain.

# Poetry

I've learned from poetry
That only prose is free.

I was taught to set my life to metered lines
When I would rather run through feathered fields
Of new mown hay
And never stop till my feet give way.
But I'm tangled in these vines of verse
And similies can be a curse.

It's easy to make rhymes.
It's harder sometimes
Not to.

# Explanation

They tell me that the stars I see
Are not necessarily there
Anymore.
They burned light years before
I was aware.

Secure in such logic
And the habit of star-filled skies,
I see no reason to answer the whys
When I get there.

# April

April you come too late.
Cinderella died at midnight
And Snow White ignores your kiss.
It's come to this:
We've grown too old for pretending
A Happy Ever After ending.

You come too late and everybody knows
That April, like princes dressed as toads,
Went out with rainbows
And yellow brick roads.

# The Road

The road we travelled side by side
Brought us together, east and west,
Ends here. And we must now decide
Which way to go, what road is best.

The miles will separate us then.
Years will pass as we recall
The road we travelled way back when
We could have stayed and had it all.

# When You Are Gone

When you are gone Iwill not speak of you.
I will talk instead of brighter days,
Amuse my friends with foolish tales
Of a happy long ago.

I will share every thought that comes to mind
Save one.
I will not speak of you.

# Fall

There's nothing left to give-
You took it all.
As long as I shall live
I'll hate the fall
And curse the cold.
The autumn gold
Now brown and brittle leaves-
Our memories.

# *Old Verse*

I know that roses are sometimes red
But the violets I've seen
Always lean
To a decidedly purple hue –
Not blue.

I point this out as an elementary example because I love you.
But love does not mean
The little lies
That common definition implies.

# Wonder

Aware of the sun glowing
On the rim of the sea –
Rising or setting –
Wondering suddenly
If it matters.

Beginnings and endings
Both take that long, shining look at the world.
And I who would run forever toward yesterday
Find instead I am letting it go,
Not knowing
If day has just begun
Or almost gone.

# The Storm

Storms that sweep across the skies,
Dark clouds changing day to night-
I hold your hand and close my eyes
To blinding bolts of flashing light.

Helpless witness inthe wake,
Threatening thunder shudders through.
No other refuge left to take,
My only hope – I cling to you.

*Sunlit days of wonder,*
*Calm days by the shore-*
*But those days of thunder*
*Come no more.*

# Unsaid

The things you do not tell,
The mysteries you hide
Are really more transparent
Than secrets you confide.

The words you will not say,
The answers incomplete –
They resonate in silence
Like a loud drum beat.

# When the Angels Come

You are growing old
Lost in memory
Of all the things you threw away
Including me.

When the angels come
And your heart is still
Pray God forgive your foolish ways –
I never will.

# Make Room

Make room for me.
I am very quiet and small.
I only need a tiny place
Near your heart –that's all.

Keep me like a picture in a locket.
Keep me like a penny in your pocket.

Make room for shells the ocean brings.
Take care of birds with broken wings.
Don't throw away small quiet things.
Make room,
Make room for me.

# Despair

I would not notice if the four horse men camped here –
So great my sorrow
And my need.
No difference to me if the world ends
In catastrophe
Or merciful sleep.
I will not meet tomorrow
With hope or fear.
There is no salvation and no sin.

I do not care
If my body dies to feed a fragrant rose.
No longer guilty of even prayer
I only weep
At the loss of wonder since I've grown old.
What does it matter
When the heart is cold
Where
The soul goes.

# Fences

I wish we had made rules,
Secured our separate selves
With barbed boundaries
And keep out signs,
Instead of trampling careless
Through the gardens of our minds.

# Regret

You find me here like sunlight,
Wind and rain
Giving warm and free.
The day is dear and shining bright
Till you look again toward the coming night
And lose the day and me.

When I forget to be there
And you trace
My footstep in the sand,
You will regret not taking care
Of the rain in my face
And the wind in my hair
And the sunlight in my hand.

# Break-up

I know it's time to end this
When I decide just how.
Maybe after one last kiss –
No, I won't do it now.

The day has come to say adieu.
The choice is very clear.
But look, that's where I first met you –
I cannot end it here.

A year is long enough to try.
I'll soon learn to forget.
Oh I will end it by and by –
But I won't do it yet.

Our break-up is a certainty.
The only question *when*.
Perhaps I'll wait till you leave me–
Yes, I will end it then.

# Revenge

I met the devil along the way.
"How do you do," said I.
"I'm looking for mischief this fine day,
Totempt a passerby."

"Then tarry not with this sad lass
For one more evil than you
Owns my soul. So let me pass.
There's no more you can do."

"Tell me more about this one.
I beg this favor give,"
He said. And I, oh, just for fun –
I told him where you live.

# Sounds

Listen to the sounds of love –
A halleluja heart
Singing like an angel choir
Joyful at the start.

Harmonic harp and chorus chime,
Laughter like a bell
Ringing clear throughout the world
Proclaiming all is well.

At last the cries of agony
Writhing in the pain.
The slamming of a final door,
The teardrops sound like rain.

Listen to the sounds of love
An almost silent cry,
The quiet breaking of aheart,
A whispered word, *goodbye*.

# Democracy

Democratic at its birth
Love seeks counsel from the Wise.
Truth speaks up for what it's worth
And Intellect replies.

Reverent Soul, with goodintent,
Overruled by Passion strong,
Surging, bold and confident
Till Reason rules it wrong.

The Senses guess. But in the end
Theruling monarch overrides.
Mind and Body recommend.
The tyrant Heart decides.

# January

We bought our January coats
Before we heard of June.
And made our morning promises
Without a thought of noon.

We watched the tattered year go by
The way all worn things do.
But it was wonderful and warm
When it was new.

# Wisteria

You planted wisteria,
Fragile cuttings from your home.
I'll see them bloom by spring next year
If I'm still here.

I planted dreams,
Fragile cuttings from my heart.
By spring next year you'll see them die.
And so will I.
And so will I.

# *Another*

An other holiday season is here,
I wait for your voice on the phone.
A long distance call full of good cheer
Then Christmas and New Year's alone.

Another tribute to Auld Lang Syne,
A toast to the year gone by –
A year that I traded for roses and wine
And all of the tears I could cry.

Another Christmas alone by the tree,
A cold gift left at my door
Ordered online –just like me–
Payment in full for your whore.

# You Will Not Know

You will not know for a day or two that I have gone;
Crossed over to a place you thought that only you could go
Undetected.
A few more peaceful nights will pass before the dawn
When come the snowflake memories floating, drifting,
swirling slow, Unexpected.

Close the door against the cold,
Know the years have made you old.
I disappear like melting snow.
But for awhile you will not know.

# Aware

Caught in the sameness
And choked by the similarity of days that drag us
Round this well-worn periphery,
I sense a sudden ending
Or at least a lack of strength to go on.

Like rats in the barn we never see
But know are there
Somewhere
Out back of our lives
Set on destruction
The insidious villains of habit and monotony
Are gnawing.

# Funeral

Our love deserves a funeral.
It has been too dear
To let it lie
Without a shroud.
Our love has been too proud
To die
Indignantly.

Something of you and something of me
Is left here.
Some prayer should be said
Some music heard
When love is dead.

Mark this moment with one stone word
Say goodbye.

# *Look*

Look at your big bed
Large enough for two.
Only one lies there instead –
You.

Look around your room.
I wonder if you see
An apparition in that tomb –
Me.

Look inside your mind
Like a book you've read.
All the dreams you left behind –
Dead.

# Description

It has not always been warm as a fireside
Or as bright.
This love we share has not always made us glad.
There have been times I thought the light
Of day would never find us.

It has never been totally sane
Nor absolutely mad.
No matter what we tried
Some random wind would dare
Remind us it will end.

It has not been sunshine or rain
Good or bad.
But it has always been
Consistently
Sad.

# The Web

Sedentary, solitary, cruising cyber-space,
Photo after photo, face after face,
Profiles prolific all about the same.
There's irony –it's called a*user*name.
See how many out there, honest, true and smart.
I might as well go buy one at the local WalMart.
Seductive and addictive, click after click.
A flirt to a favorite might do the trick.
Look, here's a message from one I'd like to meet.
All the ones I've met before –delete, delete, delete.
So boot up the computer and rev up the rom.
I'm lonely and I'm looking for *Love.com*.

# Retirement

When Iwas young and dreaming
Of what would come to be,
I saw myself grown very old
And loved by family.

Quiet, unobtrusive,
Rocking in my chair.
They would look inside my room
And see me sleeping there.

Like agentle candle
Glowing in the night.
They'd smile and say, "She's lovely
Sitting in that light".

How did I grow older?
When did I retire?
They left me unattended –
I set the house afire.

# He

I try to believe
For my love is true.
But I know he will leave
Because men do.
He'll see another and he will stray.
Without a word, he'll go away.

I try to plan,
I try to prepare –
But he is a man
And men don't care.
No matter what I do or say,
I know I cannot make him stay.

# I Will Be Brave

I will be brave and say goodbye.
I'll force a smile, my head held high,
Leave with dignity and pride
Holding all the tears inside.
I will be brave. I will not cry.

I will be wise on our last day
For I've rehearsed the words I'll say.
And I will play the perfect part.
You will not hear my breaking heart.
I will be wise. I will not stay.

I will be strong as time goes by.
I can forget you if I try.
Erase your voice, your smile, your face.
Another love will take your place.
I will be strong. I will not die.

# Innocent

You are not altogether damned for this
Though you stand accused
And unrepentant.
No doubt
The Almighty metes out
A measure of mercy equivalent to mine.
Your careless step unleashed an avalanche of earth
Covering all things green.
And when the floods came, you stood and gazed
Into the drowning canyon
Wondering.
You –the gifted –tread onthe innocent
Unaware and uncaring that they bow to you.
Blessed and bruised
By your hand,
Baptized by your kiss,
We, the weaker, wiser things, make way for arrogance.
Detached, unknowing and amazed
You see the suffering you cause
Give birth to Beauty.

# Goodbye

Spring will not come for you again.
You will lie down in winter and gather dust.
And this indifferent world will not remember
As I must.

Passing through the grief and pain
Leaving one world for another,
Wait, forgive, watch over me,
My mother.

# The Wait

I was surprised I did not die when you died.
You made it look so easy. And I tried
To stop my beating heart and hold my breath,
My arms out stretched to welcome Death.

But Death did not take me. Instead
He comes each night to my bed
To offer his cold company
And take a little part of me.

# The Gift

Grief becomes familiar
Like the comfort of old clothes.
Tomorrow, the intrusive
Uninvited guest
Brings Hope, life's compensating rose–
Beautiful and tempting. But I know
If I accept it, I must let you go.

# Hearts

Young hearts can be broken
For time will ease the pain.
Whatever lies are spoken,
The young will love again.

Age will take the best part
As days come to an end.
And when you break an old heart
There is no time to mend.

# Death

Death is never far away.
And Iwould not remind you
Except you look so sure
As if it were your
Life to decide.

If this is not enough
To put to rest your pride,
Consider Love, Death's otherside,
That takes our little span of time
And lays waste all our plans.

For in our hands
Is neither joy nor peace
Nor even the promise of another day.
And Death is never, ever far away.

# Cowards

We have outmaneuvered and outrun
Most of the slings and arrows so far
By standing still
Or taking small steps.
But that does not mean we can make promises
Or plan along trip
Or even suggest
A relationship.

Brave words –friends, love, and tomorrow –
For cowards such as we
To throw at fate.

Times like this when we feel safe
I forget the troublesome sea
And long for sleep
And the simple courage
To let it be.

# Mother's Day

*So I go running through my life, stumbling over things I had
forgotten were there.
I still select a card for your special day and choose
Violets for your grave.
I still look for a letter.
And go on living no worse and no better
Than before.
But when I lose
You are not there anymore.
The world is not the certain place I knew
When you were here.
I wonder if you see what Iam doing. I believe you see why
From your new perspective.
But Heaven is so high
And far away from me.
I still wait for your call.
The years I could have turned to you –knowing that I could –
You understand
I know you understood.
So I go running through my life and reaching for your hand
Lest I fall.*

# For Don

When I came home and found you there, eyes closed, still,
Like agiant oak suddenly felled by one swift blow.
Why didn't you call, I asked.
I knew you'd come, you said.
And they tried to save you while I watched and waited
through the days and nights
That seemed like an endless dream.
Until the end
When frail and helpless
You simply went away.

My friends stood by
When the men in Sunday suits gently carried you wrapped in
a blue velvet shroud.
Goodbye, sweet boy.
The only words left to say.
Till the night you came and danced with me
In a dream that was more real than sorrow.
You were smiling and the music was the most beautiful I have
ever heard.

*You came to let me know that you are happy and young and whole again.*
*You came to bring me peace.*
*I felt your arms around me. I felt your love.*
*Of course I knew you'd come.*
*I knew you'd come, I said.*

# *Your Name*

I know your name.
I know your name.
I've been waiting all my life for the wind to tell me who.
I still don't know where
Or why or when
Or even how to begin.
But I do know now
That you
Are really there.
And the world is not the same.

I know your name.

# *Quiet*

*You are*
*A place I go*
*To be alone.*

*For quiet moments*
*When words*
*Are like waiting birds*
*On a bare branch.*

# Choice

There is a rich man, there is a king
Who offers a kingdom, who gives me a ring.
I could live in his castle and travel a far
While servants bring truffles and rich caviar.
I could drink sweet wine, sleep in a bed
With goose-down pillows under my head.
Riches abundant, everything dear
Could be mine if I choose to stay here.

*I would live in a hollow tree*
*If you wanted me,*
*Eat wild berries, drink the dew,*
*To be with you.*

# Sunrise

I have watched the sun rise and set so many times
I should be used to it by now.
But your coming is still beautiful to me
And your going is always a little death.

# *Journey's End*

When I hear your voice,
I hear no other sound.
When I see your face,
All others fade from memory.
When you walk with me,
It does not matter where we go.
When you hold my hand,
You also hold my heart.
You are the reason for life's journey,
My final destination.
When I am in your arms,
I am home.

# Christmas

I'll save December for you.
Christmas is for giving
And I've with held the best.
I bought the sun of summer
And all my springs are put away
For Christmas Day.

I journeyed through January
And suffered June
Holding fast the loveliest
To give you last.

So late we find the perfect things;
The gentle friend,
A place to rest,
A winter home.

*This year is gift-wrapped and I wait*
*Hoping you will share*
*This final joy.*
*I cannot bear*
*The end alone.*

*I'll save December for you.*
*Please be there.*

www.ingramcontent.com/pod-product-compliance
Lightning Source LLC
Chambersburg PA
CBHW050903120626
46554CB00003B/996